DOMINOES

T0055081

V is for Vampire

LEVEL TWO   700 HEADWORDS

OXFORD

UNIVERSITY PRESS

Great Clarendon Street, Oxford, OX2 6DP, United Kingdom

Oxford University Press is a department of the University of Oxford.
It furthers the University's objective of excellence in research, scholarship,
and education by publishing worldwide. Oxford is a registered trade
mark of Oxford University Press in the UK and in certain other countries

© Oxford University Press 2013

The moral rights of the author have been asserted

First published in Dominoes 2013

2017 2016 2015

10 9 8 7 6 5 4

ISBN: 978 0 19 424983 6   Book
ISBN: 978 0 19 424967 6   Book and MultiROM Pack

MultiROM not available separately

Printed in China

This book is printed on paper from certified and well-managed sources

ACKNOWLEDGEMENTS

Illustrations by: Matteo Pincelli/Milan Illustrations Agency.

The series editors wish to express their thanks to Hardy Griffin for his helpful comments
on the story.

The publisher would like to thank the following for their permission to reproduce photographs: Corbis
pp.54 (Beach of Long Bay/Massimo Borchi/Atlantide Phototravel/Atlantide Phototravel),
56 (Joseph Sheridan Le Fanu/Hulton-Deutsch Collection); iStockphoto p.38 (Computer
screen/Dean Turner); Kobal Collection p.57 (Dracula: Bram Stoker's Dracula/Zoetrope/
Columbia Tri-Star/Nelson, Ralph Jr).

DOMINOES

Series Editors: Bill Bowler and Sue Parminter

V is for Vampire

Lesley Thompson

Illustrated by Matteo Pincelli

Lesley Thompson was born in Newcastle-upon-Tyne, in the North of England, but she moved to Spain some years ago, and now lives near Alicante. She loves reading, the cinema, music, laughing with her friends, and looking at the sea. She also enjoys walking in the countryside in England and Spain, and one day she hopes to walk the Camino de Santiago in northern Spain. Lesley has also written *Lisa's Song*, *Deep Trouble*, *The Real McCoy and Other Ghost Stories*, and *Zombie Attack!* and has adapted *Twenty Thousand Leagues under the Sea* and *The Secret Agent* in the Dominoes series.

OXFORD
UNIVERSITY PRESS

BEFORE READING

1 Match the pictures with the descriptions of the people. Use a dictionary to help you.

- **a** ☐ Ed Valdemar, an old lawyer.
- **b** ☐ George and Anne Ballantine, past owners of Ballantine's fashion house.
- **c** ☐ Angie Ballantine, George and Anne's daughter.
- **d** ☐ Don Ballantine, Angie's brother.
- **e** ☐ Vera Donato, a friend of the Ballantine family.
- **f** ☐ Viktor Sarav, a new worker at Ballantine's.
- **g** ☐ Mylene Lavine, a young woman from Canada.
- **h** ☐ Sasha Demidov, a Russian fashion designer.

2 What do you think happens in *V is for Vampire*? Complete the sentences with the names from Activity 1.

- **a** .... and his wife .... die in a plane crash not long before the story begins.
- **b** .... explains that Ballantine's belongs to Angie and Don.
- **c** .... helps her friends' children with the business.
- **d** .... comes from Bulgaria to work at Ballantine's.
- **e** .... has a car accident on the way to his sister's house.
- **f** .... falls in love with Viktor.
- **g** Something terrible happens to .... and her friend ....

Compare your ideas with a partner.

Chapter 1 – A famous business

Ed Valdemar looked down at the papers in front of him and then at the other people round the long table. Angie Ballantine, a quiet woman of twenty-five, sat across the table from him. She had a beautiful face, but just then she was tired, and her eyes were red. Her brother Don, who was two years older than her, sat next to her. He was worried, and he was watching his sister carefully. Vera Donato – a woman of forty-five with dark hair and a strong, **confident** face – sat on Valdemar's left.

'This is a difficult day for all of us,' Valdemar began in his deep voice. 'Don and Angie have lost their mother and father in a terrible accident. Vera has lost her friends and business **partners**. As an old friend also, and the Ballantine family's **lawyer** for many years, I want to make this as easy as possible for all of you. So let's begin. You are here to listen to the reading of George and Anne Ballantine's **will**.'

confident sure of yourself

partner someone who owns a business with other people

lawyer someone who works to help people with the law

will the paper that says which people you want to have your money when you die

become
(*past* **became, become**) to begin to be

future the time that will come

fashion house a business that makes and sells clothes

board of directors a group of people who look after a business

The old lawyer was silent for a minute. Then he began to read aloud from the papers in front of him. His voice, at first quiet and shaking, **became** louder and stronger. Angie began to cry softly while she listened to Valdemar reading the words of the will. Don held her hand. Vera listened sadly, and looked at the large photograph on the wall of Anne and George in happier days. George – a tall man with brown hair – had his arm round his wife, and they were smiling.

The reading of the will did not take long. The Ballantines often talked to their children and Vera about their plans for the **future**, so there were no big surprises. They were leaving everything to Angie and Don. There were houses in different countries, expensive cars and pictures, and a lot of money. Most importantly, Ballantine's – the famous New York **fashion house** – was now in the young people's hands.

'Now, you know that Vera is already on the **board of directors**,' Valdemar went on. 'This doesn't change. The three of you will now work together as partners. If anything happens to Don and Angie, the business will go to Vera. George and Anne wanted things this way. And it's my job to do what they wanted. Are there any questions? If not, let's finish here. I think that all of us need a rest now.'

Without another word, Valdemar put the papers into his bag and stood up. While he and the others were slowly leaving the room, he thought for the hundredth time about the strange accident that killed his friends. Was it only a month ago? George and Anne were flying to Boston in their small plane. George was the **pilot**. They were flying over open country when things went terribly wrong, and the plane suddenly fell to the ground and crashed. The police said that something was caught in the plane's **engines**, but it was difficult to see **exactly** what it was. Large numbers of birds – or **bats** – were not usual in that place, and nobody could explain it. George and Anne often flew to Boston, and they knew the journey well. It was dark, but the weather was fine. So why exactly did they crash? Valdemar shook his head. Was it just bad luck?

pilot this person flies a plane

engine the machine in a plane that makes it move

exactly really

bat a small animal that flies at night

Later that day, Angie and Don met Vera in her office to talk about the future of Ballantine's. Angie walked worriedly around the room, a coffee cup in her hand.

'Oh, what are we going to do? You must help us, Vera,' said Angie. 'Don and I are new to the business, and we have a lot to learn. Mom and Dad worked all their lives to make Ballantine's into a famous fashion house. I don't want to lose it all now.'

'That won't happen,' said Vera confidently. 'I worked hard for your father and mother, and I'll work hard for you, too. Ballantine's is strong and it can be stronger. I'm already thinking about our next big **fashion show** in Milan. I'm thinking about wonderful suits, little dresses, big hats, and great bags and shoes. I see unusual colours for Ballantine's this summer, bright red, dark grey – and black! I can see it now! It's going to be the biggest and best fashion show of all time!'

'Mmm, that sounds exciting, Vera. But how exactly are we going to do it?' asked Don. 'Ballantine's wasn't doing so well when Mom and Dad died. It was starting to lose some of its best people. I know that my mother and father were talking about changing some things. What can you tell us about all that?'

'I know about it, of course,' answered Vera. 'Things weren't going too well, and we've lost a few good people in the last months. **Maybe** our **image** has become boring over the last few years. You can't rest in this business. We need new faces and new **ideas** around the place. We must look for people to bring new life to the business. New blood. There are hundreds of bright young people in New York who would really like to work for Ballantine's so I'm not worried. We just have to find them.' Vera spoke confidently, and her words gave Angie new hope. Her brother was not so sure.

'Maybe you're right,' said Don. 'You know all the important people in the world of **fashion**. But I have friends in the business, too. If you don't mind, I'm going to start right now and make a few phone calls.' Don looked lovingly at his sister.

fashion show
people can see
the newest
clothes at this

maybe perhaps

image a picture
that people have
in their head of a
business

idea something
that you think

fashion clothes
that are new and
interesting for
many people

'Take it easy, Angie, and stop worrying! I'll see you later. OK?'

Without another word to Vera, Don hurried out of the room. Vera looked sadly after him. With his brown hair and blue eyes, the young man was very like his father.

Angie knew that Vera felt sad, and she tried to help the older woman. 'You're not alone, Vera,' she said. 'Don and I learn fast. I'm not very confident, I know, but I'm ready to work hard.'

Vera smiled, but said nothing. The girl was young and she didn't know much about the fashion world. She needed all the help that Vera could give her.

In her head, Vera spoke silently to her dead friends. 'Dear George and Anne, I'll never forget you, and I'll always be here for Angie and Don. You said that I was the best. And with my help and everyone's hard work, Ballantine's will soon be the best fashion house in the world. Nothing – and nobody – will stand in the way of that.'

READING CHECK

1 Are these sentences true or false? Tick the boxes.

		True	False
a	Angie's parents die before the story begins.	☑	☐
b	Ed Valdemar was a friend of George and Anne's.	☐	☐
c	George and Anne were poor when they died.	☐	☐
d	Vera wants to work hard for Ballantine's.	☐	☐
e	Angie and Don need Vera's help.	☐	☐
f	Ed Valdemar never thinks about the plane crash.	☐	☐
g	Vera thinks that they need to change things at Ballantine's.	☐	☐
h	Ballantine's next fashion show will be in Paris.	☐	☐

2 Match the first and second parts of the sentences.

a 'This is a difficult day for all of us,'

b 'So why exactly did they crash?'

c 'Don and I are new to the business,'

d 'How exactly are we going to change our image?'

e 'We need new faces and new ideas,'

f 'I'll never forget you,'

1 Vera says to her dead friends.

2 Don asks Vera.

3 Vera says to Don and Angie.

4 Valdemar says to the people round the table.

5 Valdemar asks himself.

6 Angie says to Vera.

ACTIVITIES

WORD WORK

Use the words in the plane to complete the sentences.
They all come from Chapter 1.

Words in the plane: maybe, exactly, confident, engines, pilot, future, fashion show, bats, partner, will, image, become, ideas, lawyer

a After the accident, they needed a ....*lawyer*.... to help them.

b A lot of little .... fly around here at night.

c I don't understand you very well. What .... do you mean?

d He's always good at thinking of new ....

e The clothes must be ready in time for the .... in London.

f Their parents left a lot of money to them in their ....

g No one knows what will happen next. The .... is unclear.

h I'm not sure, but I think that .... she's afraid of him.

i She's a very .... person who knows what she wants.

j You've worked very well here. Would you like to be a .... in our business?

k Her son wants to .... a doctor.

l People think of our company as old and boring. We need to change our ....

m The accident happened after something flew into both the .... of the plane.

n The .... died in the plane crash.

GUESS WHAT

Which of these things do you think happen in the next chapter? Tick four boxes.

a ☐ Some new people begin to work at Ballantine's.

b ☐ Ed Valdemar marries Vera.

c ☐ Don kills Viktor.

d ☐ Angie becomes the new face of Ballantine's.

e ☐ Viktor and Vera do not agree.

f ☐ Angie hits Vera.

g ☐ Angie calls Valdemar.

h ☐ Don and Viktor go to Bulgaria.

Chapter 2 – The new crowd

Two weeks later, things were already changing at Ballantine's. A crowd of new people, with exciting ideas, were working there.

One of them was **Mylene**, a Canadian girl who laughed a lot and was full of life. She was their new **buyer**, and she had a wonderful eye for interesting colours.

Sasha came from a fashion house in Russia. His **designs** were new and different. And he worked well with Mylene.

Ballantine's was paying them a lot of money. 'But they'll make a lot more money for Ballantine's,' Vera said to herself.

Maybe the most interesting of the new crowd was Viktor Sarav, Ballantine's new image **consultant**. He was tall and **pale**. He always dressed in black and wore dark glasses. Viktor was funny and **charming**. He came from Bulgaria, and spoke many different languages. His ideas for changing the **company** image were exciting. He was unknown to Vera, which was surprising because she knew nearly everyone in the fashion world. But he knew a lot about fashion and business. Angie and Don liked him immediately when they **interviewed** him. Vera was not so sure. He was just as confident as she was, and she really did not like that.

'He's great, Vera,' said Angie. 'Let's give him the job before another fashion house takes him.'

'Maybe you're right,' said Vera. She didn't feel very comfortable with Viktor – she couldn't explain why. But he *was* good at his job.

Viktor worked hard and fast to change Ballantine's. Men and women liked him. Mylene secretly **fell in love** with him. He explained things for hours to Angie and Don, and with his help, they began to understand the business better. Vera learned from him, too – and she gave him more work. Soon the company's image was better than ever.

Mylene /mɪˈlɛn/

buyer a person who buys things for a business

design when you plan and draw things before they are made

consultant a person who helps a business when they are having trouble with something

pale without a lot of colour

charming nice to other people

company a business

interview to ask questions for somebody to answer

fall (*past* **fell**) **in love** to begin to love

'We did the right thing when we gave Viktor the job,' said Don. Vera had to agree with him.

Every Wednesday morning, everybody at Ballantine's met to talk about the past week and to explain their new ideas.

Viktor first spoke of his new plan for Ballantine's on one of these Wednesday mornings.

'Listen, everybody,' he began. 'I have a new idea. Look.'

He showed everyone a large photograph of Angie in a white dress with the words *The Face of Ballantine's* under it.

'That's me at the company party last year!' said Angie. 'Where did you find that photo?'

'In the company **magazine**,' replied Viktor. 'Of course, I put the words underneath.' Then he turned to the others and went on. 'I think that you'll agree – Angie has a great face. The camera loves her – and she *is* Ballantine's. In future, I want to use her as the face of the fashion house. She'll be on the front of our magazine, in all our **publicity**, always wearing our clothes! Look at her – clever, rich, and beautiful. She's the best of all **models** for us to use.'

magazine a thin book with news and a lot of photos

publicity information that makes people want to buy something

model a person who wears clothes to show them to other people

The Face of Ballantine's

9

Everyone was silent for a minute. Then they all began talking at the same time. A lot of people agreed with Viktor.

'What do you think, Angie? Will you be our new model?' asked Viktor, smiling at her.

'I'm not sure,' said Angie, her face becoming red. 'I ... I've never done anything like that before.'

'It's a great idea,' said Don. 'People will remember Angie's face and name. And our clothes are just right for her.'

Then Vera spoke.

'We must be careful with this,' she said. 'Firstly, it's going to mean more work for Angie. Secondly, won't it give the wrong idea about Ballantine's? Aren't we telling people that we're a small company with no money? If Angie's face is on all our publicity, they'll just think that we're trying to save on models' bills! We don't want that!'

Again everyone was silent for a minute.

Then Don replied. 'I don't think that what you're saying is really true, Vera. Everybody knows that Ballantine's always spends money when it's necessary. You want the company to do well, don't you?'

Vera said nothing, but her face was red and angry.

'So, do we all agree? Will Angie be the new face of Ballantine's?' asked Viktor brightly. 'Yes, of course!' nearly everyone in the room replied excitedly.

Vera was silent. She did not agree, but what could one person do against so many?

That afternoon, Angie went into Vera's office to talk.

'Are you OK?' she asked. 'I know that you didn't agree with Viktor this morning, but I think that his idea's good. I'm just not exactly sure about being a model!'

'I'm worried about this, Angie. Nobody ever listens carefully to what Viktor's saying – because he's so charming,' said Vera.

'He knows what he's doing, Vera. I'm sure of that. But if you think that it's a bad idea, I won't do it,' replied Angie.

'No, no. Maybe
I'm making a mistake.
We wanted to change our image
and this is what Viktor has decided.
So let's try it,' Vera told her.

Alone in her office that evening, Angie
called Ed Valdemar and told him about Viktor
and Vera's **disagreement**.

'What do you think, Ed? Can I be the new face of
Ballantine's? I've never been a model before.'

'You're beautiful and bright, Angie,' said Valdemar. 'You just
need to be more confident. But don't ask me about the model
business – because I've no idea!'

Later, Valdemar thought more about Viktor and Vera. 'Both
of them are strange,' he said to himself. 'Poor Vera's never been
the same since George and Anne died. And Viktor's come from
nowhere and wants to change everything.' He wasn't sure
what he thought about Don, but he **cared** about Angie and the
company. 'It'll be interesting to see what happens to Ballantine's
in the future,' thought Valdemar.

disagreement
when two or more
people don't agree

care to feel
interested in, and
to worry about,
someone or
something

11

READING CHECK

Correct the mistakes in these sentences.

a   Things begin to change ~~slowly~~ *quickly* at Ballantine's.

b   Some old workers come to work at the fashion house.

c   Ballantine's is not paying these workers a lot of money.

d   Viktor, Mylene, and Sasha have some boring ideas.

e   Angie will become the new voice of Ballantine's.

f   Vera agrees with Viktor's idea about Angie.

g   Angie is very confident about being a model.

h   'People will think that Ballantine's is rich,' Vera says.

i   Angie phones Viktor because she is worried.

j   Valdemar does not care about what happens to Angie and the company.

WORD WORK

Choose the best word or phrase to complete each sentence.

a   I'm going to buy a (*magazine*) / *company* to read on the train.

b   That girl is a *design* / *model* at a famous fashion house.

c   You look very *charming* / *pale*. Do you feel OK?

d   There's a *disagreement* / *publicity* between the partners about the future of the business.

e   Without a lot of *publicity* / *consultant*, people will forget about the company.

f   Our *model* / *buyer* is going to Milan to look for clothes for our new shop.

g   He's going to *interview* / *fall in love with* ten people for the job this afternoon.

h Viktor Sarav is a *short* / *charming* man and everyone likes him.

i We need a *consultant* / *buyer* to give us a new image.

j Ballantine's is a famous New York *company* / *publicity*.

k Vera *cares about* / *interviews* the future of Ballantine's.

l Mylene *falls in love with* / *cares about* Viktor.

GUESS WHAT

What do you think these three people do in the next chapter? Tick two boxes to finish each sentence.

a Viktor …

   1 ☐ shouts at Mylene.

   2 ☐ breaks Angie's leg.

   3 ☐ tells Angie that Vera has hurt him.

b Angie …

   1 ☐ asks Viktor what happened to his head.

   2 ☐ goes to her house with Viktor.

   3 ☐ runs away with Sasha.

c Don …

   1 ☐ goes for dinner with Viktor.

   2 ☐ asks Vera about Viktor's story of the parking garage.

   3 ☐ calls Angie from his car.

Chapter 3 – Viktor is hurt

The next morning, Viktor came into the office later than usual. His face was very pale, and he was wearing his usual dark glasses. Round his head, he had a large, white **bandage**. A little blood ran down his face from under it.

Mylene was the first to see him.

'Viktor,' she cried. 'What's this? Are big bandages the latest fashion?' She put up her hand to touch Viktor's head. To her surprise, he pushed her away and shouted angrily at her, 'Don't touch me! Don't come near me! Just stay away!'

Mylene felt suddenly afraid. Why was Viktor shouting? He usually laughed when she said something like that.

'Hey,' said Sasha, one of the few people at Ballantine's who did not like Viktor. 'Don't speak to Mylene like that. Who do you think you are?'

'Ah, you'd like to know the answer to that mystery, wouldn't you?' said Viktor, laughing strangely.

Just then, Angie came out of her office.

'What's happening?' she asked everybody. 'What's all the noise about?'

'I'm sorry, Angie,' said Viktor, smiling at her. 'Mylene wanted to touch my head and I shouted at her. I'm sorry. I'm feeling really unwell this morning.'

'What happened to you?' asked Angie.

bandage a long, thin cloth that you put on your body when you are hurt

Viktor took Angie's arm and walked with her away from Mylene and Sasha. He spoke in a soft voice in her ear.

'Someone hit me on the head in the **parking garage**. I didn't want to say anything in front of the others because ...'

'What?'

'Well, I'm not sure – but I think that it was Vera who hit me. When I was lying on the ground, I saw her running away across the garage. I'm sure of it.'

Angie was **shocked**. 'What a terrible thing to happen! And you think that Vera did this! But why?'

'She's **jealous** of me. She thinks that I'm trying to take the company away from her,' said Viktor.

'So she hit you in the parking garage! I can't **believe** it,' said Angie. 'But we can find out easily. Let's look at the **CCTV camera**. That will show us exactly what happened.'

Viktor's face was suddenly **confused**. 'Oh, no,' he said quickly. 'I don't think that we need to go so far. Let's just forget about it, Angie. Vera and I have to work together. Maybe I'm wrong and it wasn't her. The garage is dark, after all. Maybe someone wanted to steal some money from me and ran away when they heard something.'

'But, Viktor, this is very worrying,' said Angie shaking her head. 'We must find out what really happened.'

Just then, the office phone rang noisily. Sasha answered it. 'It's for you, Viktor,' he shouted across the room. 'An important call from Milan.'

'Take the call, Viktor,' said Angie. 'We'll speak later.'

So Viktor took the call. And Angie went at once to see Don in his office and told him about Viktor's story.

'Hmm,' said Don. 'I can't really believe that Vera did it. But we know that she doesn't like Viktor, and I don't think that he'd **lie** about something like this. Leave things with me, Angie. I'll speak to Vera about it at once.'

Minutes later, Vera was in Don's office. She was shocked when

parking garage a big room under a building where people can leave their cars

shocked very surprised by something bad

jealous feeling angry or sad because you want to have what another person has

believe to think that something is true

CCTV camera (short for closed circuit television camera) a camera that records things that happen in a place

confused not understanding something well

lie to say something that is not true

15

Don told her about Viktor's story.

'Well, did you do it?' he asked her.

'*Hit* Viktor!' she cried. 'Don, you've known me for years. I've never hit anyone in my life. Are you **crazy**?'

'Hey there, take it easy,' said Don. 'Look, I have to ask you, Vera. You must see that.'

'He's lying, Don. Have you looked at the CCTV camera **recording** yet?'

'No, but I'm going to do that right now.'

Don went downstairs to the room that had all the CCTV camera recordings in it. While he was sitting in front of the TV, a **figure** in black with something white on its head came up silently behind him, stood there for a minute, and then went away. Don saw and heard nothing, but he felt strangely tired – and confused – after that. He watched the recording from the parking garage earlier in the day. He **gasped** in surprise at what he saw. Viktor got out of his car in the garage and walked quickly over to the nearest wall. He then hit his head really hard three times against it.

After that, he took a bandage out of his pocket and put it round his head. He was alone. Viktor was lying after all!

Don knew that he had to move fast. He decided to **erase** the recording because he did not want Angie to watch it. He knew that she liked Viktor a lot, and maybe she didn't need to see this. Then he went back to his office and wrote a letter to Ed Valdemar, telling him everything.

'Ed must know,' he thought. 'That way, if Viktor does anything to stop me, Valdemar will have the letter to use against him. And now I must tell Angie to be careful. Viktor's lied to us once, and he can do it again. We can't fully **trust** him after this.'

'I need to speak to Angie. Where is she?' Don asked Mylene when she walked past his office door.

'She left with Viktor a few minutes ago,' answered Mylene. 'They've gone to her house to look at the designs for Milan.'

Mylene spoke very unhappily. She couldn't feel the same about Viktor Sarav after what happened earlier.

Don suddenly had a very bad **feeling**. He must hurry.

On his way out of the office, he remembered to **mail** his letter to Valdemar. Then he quickly got into his car and drove down the road to Angie's house. On the way, he took his **cell phone** out of his pocket to call his sister.

erase to take away the sounds and pictures from a recording

trust to believe that someone is nice and good

feeling something that you feel inside yourself

mail to send something by mail; to post

cell phone a phone that you can carry with you

READING CHECK

Put these sentences in the correct order. Number them 1–10.

a ☐ Don erases the CCTV recording.

b ☐ Viktor tells Angie that someone hit him in the parking garage.

c ☐ Don speaks to Vera about Viktor.

d ☐ Mylene tries to touch Viktor's head.

e ☐ A black figure comes up behind Don.

f ☐ Don gets into his car and starts driving to Angie's house.

g ☐ Viktor goes into the office wearing a bandage on his head.

h ☐ Don writes a letter to Valdemar and mails it.

i ☐ Sasha shouts at Viktor.

j ☐ Don sees Viktor on the CCTV recording.

WORD WORK

1 Find seventeen words or phrases from Chapter 3 in the bandage.

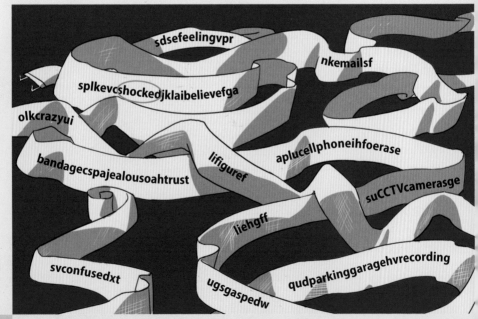

sdsefeelingvpr

nkemailsf

splkevcshockedjklaibelievefga

olkcrazyui

aplucellphoneihfoerase

bandagecspajealousoahtrust

lifiguref

suCCTVcamerasge

liehgff

svconfusedxt

ugsgaspedw

qudparkinggaragehvrecording

2 Complete the sentences with the words from Activity 1 on page 18.

a We were ...shocked... when we heard about the terrible accident.

b Can you .... that letter for me when you go out?

c I saw a .... at the window. Maybe it was John.

d You say that you didn't do it, but I don't .... you.

e He left his car in the ....

f I really think that you're .... to spend all of your work money on the very first day of every month.

g She was .... of her brother because he had everything and she had nothing.

h He burnt his hand so the nurse put a .... on it.

i Can I .... you to carry the baby without dropping her?

j Hotels often have .... outside to see who goes in and who comes out.

k My grandfather is very old, and he becomes .... when he has a lot of different things to remember.

l The police officers had a very bad .... about Nurse Smith. They knew that she was the murderer of many women in the hospital.

m When he read the news, his mouth fell open and he .... in surprise.

n I have a new .... which can also take photographs.

o We've listened to the .... of the phone call three times, but we still don't understand every word of it fully.

p Nothing that you say is true. You always .... to me.

q I'm going to .... that photograph from my camera. I don't like it.

GUESS WHAT

Which of these things do you think happens in the next chapter? Write *Yes* or *No*.

a Don has an accident. ....

b Don tells Angie about the CCTV recording. ....

c The police go to Vera's house. ....

d Vera tells the police that Viktor is a good man. ....

e Viktor tells Vera that he knows something secret about her. ....

Vera looked at the two police officers standing at her front door.

'Are you telling me that Don Ballantine is dead?' she asked them both slowly.

'Yes, I'm afraid so, Miss Donato,' said the older man. 'I'm very sorry. We know that it's a bad time, but can we come in and interview you? It won't take long.'

The men walked in at once and sat down in Vera's living room. Vera sat opposite them.

'When and where did you last see Mr Ballantine, Miss Donato?' the older policeman began.

'At the office this morning,' said Vera, her voice shaking. 'We spoke together about one of our workers.' She explained to them about Viktor, and all about his story of what happened to him in the parking garage.

'And later, Mr Ballantine drove to his sister's house?'

'Yes. I wanted to talk to him again, and Mylene – our buyer – told me that he was going to Angie's. Was it an accident?' Vera asked.

'We think so. He was driving and talking on his cell phone to his sister when it happened. He shouted something about a **huge** bat flying into the **windshield**. Then he went off the road and crashed into a tree. He died immediately,' said the policeman.

huge very big

windshield the glass at the front of a car

'Oh, poor Don – and poor Angie,' said Vera. 'First, her father and mother die in a plane crash, and now her brother dies in this car accident. It's terrible!'

'We have to ask you this, Miss Donato,' the policeman went on. 'Did anyone want to hurt Mr Ballantine, do you think?'

Vera was silent for a minute before she spoke.

'I don't trust Viktor Sarav – our image consultant. He told Angie that I hit him in the parking garage this morning. Well, I didn't do it. So we know that he lies about things.'

The younger policeman spoke now.

'But, Miss Donato, Viktor Sarav has an **alibi**. He was with Miss Ballantine at the time of the accident. Are you saying that Viktor did something to Don's car? Our men can't find anything wrong with it.'

'I don't know what he did,' said Vera slowly. 'But he did something. I can feel it.'

The older policeman shook his head.

'We need more than that,' he said. 'Feelings aren't enough when we're talking about a possible murder.'

Angie's beautiful face was pale and her eyes were really red from crying. Vera went and put her arms round the young woman.

'I'm so very sorry, Angie,' she said softly.

'Why did it happen, Vera? I can't believe it. First Mom and Dad, and now Don – it's all too much!' said Angie.

'I know. You poor girl! You're right. And both of them strange accidents, too,' Vera went on.

alibi something that shows that you were in another place at the time of a crime and so not the criminal

'What do you mean?' asked Angie.

'Well, your father was a good pilot, and Don was a good driver. The plane and the car crashed after something flew into them. The police spoke about birds or bats. It's all very strange ...'

'Stop saying things like that, Vera! They were both just terrible accidents – nothing more!' cried Angie.

'Yes, of course. I'm sorry,' said Vera softly.

She walked to one of the front windows in Angie's house and looked out of it, into the street.

'Angie,' she said, 'have you looked at the CCTV recording of the parking garage yet?'

'Yes, but there's nothing on it,' replied Angie. 'Maybe it wasn't working. I can't think about that now. But Viktor says that he was wrong about you. Now he says that a thief hit him and ran away. He wants to forget it. And he wants to **look after** me, he says. He's so kind, Vera. You know, you and Viktor are the two most important people in my life now.'

A week later, Vera was working in her office one morning when there was a sudden knock on her door. Viktor walked in confidently and smiled at her.

'How are you, Vera? I've come to say that I'm sorry about last week. I was wrong about you. Let's forget it and work together on the Milan fashion show. Poor Angie is still **weak** and can't help much, I'm afraid. We two must work harder than ever to help her and Ballantine's.'

Vera looked stonily at the young man.

'Viktor, maybe you can **fool** Angie, but you can't fool me,' she said. 'You want Ballantine's all for yourself, and nothing is going to stop you, is it?'

Viktor smiled strangely at her.

'I don't know what you're talking about. You don't have any **proof** of anything, do you? It's your word against my word. Be careful, Vera. After all, you have things to hide, don't you? Angie

look after to do things for someone, or something, that needs help

weak not strong

fool to make someone think things that are not true; a person who thinks things that are not true

proof something which shows that a thing is really true

22

can't find out about you stealing money from your dear old friends, can she now?'

Vera's face was suddenly very white.

'How did you find out about that?' she gasped.

'Don't be surprised, Vera Donato. I can "read" people like books,' said Viktor. 'So let's be friends, eh? Let's do what's best for Angie, and for Ballantine's. OK?'

Vera said 'OK' quietly. Viktor was right. She had no proof of anything, and she had a terrible secret to hide. A few years before, when her mother was in hospital, Vera 'borrowed' a lot of money from the company without telling either George or Anne. She had plans to pay it back. But after some time, when nobody said anything about the money, she forgot those plans. The company had a lot of money, and Vera thought that she was **safe**. 'How can Viktor know about it after all this time?' she said to herself. 'Maybe he'll tell Angie and Ed about the money and they'll never trust me again. I'll lose everything.'

She watched through the open door after Viktor left her office. Angie was sitting at a table by the window, looking at some designs. She was very thin and pale. Viktor walked over to her, and put his arm round her. She looked up at him, and smiled sadly. More than ever now, the poor girl needed someone to look after her.

safe when nothing bad can happen to you

23

READING CHECK

Match the first and second parts of these sentences.

a Two police officers go to Vera's house ☐ 3

b The police tell Vera that something ☐

c Angie cannot believe ☐

d Viktor tells Vera that he wants to work ☐

e Viktor knows that ☐

f Vera cannot say anything bad about Viktor ☐

g For Angie, Vera and Viktor are the two ☐

1 that her parents and brother are dead.

2 because he knows too much about her.

3 and tell her about Don's accident.

4 most important people in her life now.

5 flew into Don's windshield.

6 Vera stole money from the company.

7 harder than ever for Ballantine's.

WORD WORK

1 Find words and phrases from Chapter 4 in the bats.

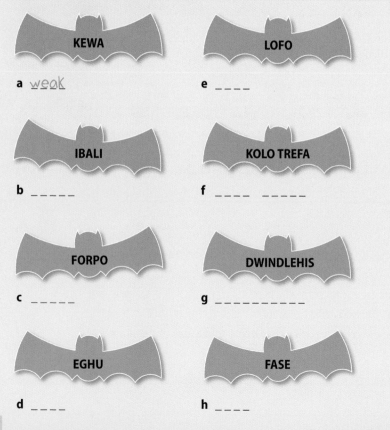

KEWA

a weak

LOFO

e _ _ _ _

IBALI

b _ _ _ _ _

KOLO TREFA

f _ _ _ _   _ _ _ _ _

FORPO

c _ _ _ _ _

DWINDLEHIS

g _ _ _ _ _ _ _ _ _ _

EGHU

d _ _ _ _

FASE

h _ _ _ _

2 Complete the sentences with the words and phrases from Activity 1 on page 24.

a You think that he stole the money, but do you have any ..... proof .....?

b Vera is a strong person, but Angie is ....

c Three thousand people live in that .... building over there.

d I can't see through the .... because it's raining heavily.

e Can you .... the children when I go out later?

f Where were you at 12 o'clock? Do you have an .... for the time of the crime?

g Vera felt .... from the police because her crime happened a long time ago.

h Viktor cannot .... Vera. She knows that he wants everything for himself.

GUESS WHAT

What do you think happens in the next chapter? Complete the sentences with the people's names.

Angie

Sasha

Viktor

Mylene

Vera

a .... is a model at the fashion show in Milan.

b .... says that he has an old house in Bulgaria.

c .... tries to find out more about Viktor's past life.

d Back in New York, Vera learns that .... and .... are dead.

Chapter 5 – A vacation in Bulgaria

That year's spring and summer fashion show in Milan was in late October. It was a great **success** for Ballantine's. Everybody loved their unusual summer clothes in black, red, and grey. Angie was a beautiful model with her pale face and large, sad eyes. Viktor and Vera were in Milan with Angie. When the fashion show finished, the three of them met back at their hotel.

'Let's drink to Ballantine's, and to a very successful future,' said Viktor, with his glass in his hand.

'To the future,' they all said.

'And now you must rest for a few weeks, Angie,' said Vera. 'Your face is so tired.'

'I agree,' said Viktor. 'I have an old family house near Varna in Bulgaria. Why don't you go there? It's a nice, quiet place. The old **housekeeper** can look after you. Vera can go, too.'

'Oh, yes, let's do that, Vera,' cried Angie. 'I've always wanted to see Viktor's family house.'

More than anything, Vera wanted to hurry back to New York. 'What will Viktor do there, alone at Ballantine's? He's planning something,' she said to herself. But she had to agree to this vacation. Viktor knew too much about her, and she couldn't say 'no'. 'And maybe I'll learn something about *him* when I'm there in Bulgaria,' she thought.

'We'll take two weeks' **vacation** in Varna,' she said, smiling at Angie, 'And then go back to Ballantine's.'

success when you get what you want

housekeeper a woman who looks after someone's house

vacation days when you do not have to go to work

Not much happened during their vacation. Viktor's house was old and falling down, but the old housekeeper was kind and looked after them well. She spoke a little English.

In the first days of their vacation, Vera tried to ask the old woman about Viktor's past life. 'When did he come here? What happened to his family?' she asked.

But the housekeeper just shook her head and smiled. Maybe she didn't understand. After that, Vera asked her no more questions. There were also, she saw, no old photographs or pictures of the family in the house to help her.

Angie slept a lot in the garden, and soon Vera too began to rest. Viktor called to say that everything was going well at the office. So Vera read her magazines, went for long walks, and tried to forget about work.

After two weeks, Angie was still pale but she felt better. Vera was in a hurry to get back to Ballantine's. Both women wanted to see Viktor again, but for different **reasons**. Vera wanted to stop his plans for changing the company. Angie was falling in love with him.

———————

'I knew it! Viktor's changed everything,' said Vera to herself. She was back in her office in New York, and she was shocked.

'Oh, yes, I've found some new people, and some of the old crowd have gone. They weren't working well,' said Viktor when she asked him about it. 'It's a stronger company now. We mustn't be afraid of changing things.'

'But why aren't Sasha and Mylene here?' asked Vera. 'You always said that they worked very well.'

The smile suddenly left Viktor's face. 'Something terrible happened, Vera. They found Sasha and Mylene dead in a back street last week. There was blood everywhere. The police think that it was murder. They were near a **club**, *Black's*. It's always full of strange people. I think that Sasha and Mylene were drinking there just before they died. I didn't tell you about it

reason why you do something

club a place where people listen to music and dance

27

because you were on vacation and needed to rest.'

'And do you know anything about their deaths, Viktor?' asked Vera.

'No,' replied Viktor. 'Nothing at all. It's terribly sad, but New York can be a **violent** place. You know that, Vera.'

Vera walked back to her office. 'I don't believe him,' she said to herself. She immediately called **Fleur**, a young designer who was working at a **rival** fashion house.

'Hi, Fleur,' she said. 'How are things, dear? I've just heard the terrible news about Sasha and Mylene. You knew them both well, didn't you?'

'Yes,' said Fleur. 'And I was with them at *Black's* that night – just before they died.'

'Was there anything unusual about them?' asked Vera.

'No. They were happy, laughing, and dancing,' explained Fleur. 'But I remember one strange thing. They spoke to Viktor Sarav. He arrived while we were there. He wasn't happy to see Sasha and Mylene. I think that he was angry with them about something. He was shouting at them. But there was no fighting in the club. Soon after that, Sasha and Mylene left.'

'Did Viktor leave with them?' Vera asked, interestedly.

'Not long after,' Fleur replied. 'Why?'

'Oh, nothing. I'm just trying to understand exactly what happened that night,' Vera explained.

'I see. You know,' Fleur went on, 'I think that Sasha was in love with Angie Ballantine, and that Viktor was jealous of him. That was maybe the reason for their disagreement.'

'Yes, maybe. Thanks, Fleur,' said Vera.

She put the phone down, held her head in her hands, and thought for a minute. Then she called Angie who was at home, still tired after the long plane journey back from Bulgaria. Vera gave her all the news about Ballantine's. She also told her about Sasha and Mylene's deaths.

'I didn't want to say this to you, Angie, but I must. Viktor is dangerous. Violent things happen around him all the time. You must be careful. I'm very worried for you.'

'Don't worry about me,' answered Angie. 'For me, Viktor is strong, not dangerous. He's done so much for Ballantine's in the past months. He cares about me, Vera. You can't say anything to change that. Please leave him alone. Like he says, New York can be violent, and terrible things happen. I trust him. You must trust him, too. I'm finishing this call now, before you say anything more against Viktor.'

With that, Angie ended the call. Vera put the phone down slowly. She suddenly felt very tired and alone.

ACTIVITIES

READING CHECK

Correct nine more mistakes in the story.

Viktor, Vera, and Angie go to an important fashion show in ~~London~~. Milan After the show, Angie is very tired and Viktor tells her about his boat in Bulgaria. Angie and Vera agree to go there on vacation for seven weeks. In Bulgaria, Vera tries to speak to the housekeeper about Viktor, but the old man does not understand her. Both Vera and Angie want to go back to New York as late as possible.

Back at the office, Viktor has changed few things. He tells Vera the good news about Sasha and Mylene. They died after a night out at *Black's*. Their dead bodies were found inside the club, on the ground. Vera does not believe Viktor's story. She calls Fleur, a young writer who knew Sasha and Mylene. Fleur tells Vera that Viktor was at the club on the night of her friends' deaths. She thinks that Sasha and Viktor maybe had a disagreement over Angie. Vera tells Angie that she must trust Viktor, but Angie doesn't listen because she loves Viktor.

WORD WORK

1 Complete the crossword with seven words from Chapter 5.

Crossword clues:
1 S
2 C
3 V
4 HOUSEKEEPER
5 R
6 R
7 VAT

30

ACTIVITIES

2 Use the words in Activity 1 on page 30 to complete the sentences.

a She worked all her life as a . . . . housekeeper . . . . for a rich Italian family.

b The company was a big . . . . at the Milan fashion show.

c She's very tired and she needs to go on a . . . .

d I like that new . . . . in town. They play great music there.

e I have a good . . . . for leaving my job. I don't enjoy the work.

f The fashion house lost a lot of their business to a . . . . company.

g Be careful. That man is . . . . , and he has a knife.

GUESS WHAT

What do you think happens to Vera in the next chapter?
Tick one box in a, b, c, and d.

a Vera learns that …
   1 ☐ nobody knows how old Viktor really is.
   2 ☐ Viktor's real name is different.
   3 ☐ Viktor comes from a very old family.

b Vera goes to Viktor's apartment …
   1 ☐ to speak to him about Angie.
   2 ☐ to find out more about him.
   3 ☐ to kill him if she can.

c When Vera is at Viktor's apartment, …
   1 ☐ he calls her on his cell phone.
   2 ☐ he tells her that he loves her.
   3 ☐ he arrives and finds her there.

d Vera learns that …
   1 ☐ Angie is dead.
   2 ☐ Viktor is going to marry Angie.
   3 ☐ Angie is looking for another job.

Chapter 6 – Vera is too late

In the following weeks, Vera became **obsessed** with Viktor Sarav. Was he really as bad as she thought? She needed to find some proof somewhere to show it. But where? And how?

One night, she stayed behind after everyone left the office. First, she went to Viktor's computer and turned it on. But it showed her nothing interesting about him.

Next, she went back to her office and used her computer to look on the **Internet**. She quickly wrote the name 'Viktor Sarav' and waited. A lot of news stories about him came up on the **screen**.

'Ah, that's better!' she said to herself.

There was some news about his work for Ballantine's and the success of the Milan fashion show. But there was nothing about his time in Bulgaria or in any other fashion houses. Then Vera saw something strange. How old was Viktor exactly? Nobody knew! In some of the stories he was in his twenties, but more often he was older. Some of the stories talked about a man who was over sixty! How was that possible? His face was young and he moved like a young man. Was he lying about that, too?

'This man is a real mystery,' Vera said to herself. 'What exactly is behind all of this?'

obsessed always thinking about the same thing

Internet you use a computer and a phone line to find different things on this

screen something flat at the front of a computer or TV on which you can see things

Vera waited a few more days. In February, Viktor went to London for an important **fall** and winter fashion show. 'He's away for five days and is coming back on the weekend. It's now or never,' thought Vera. 'I must find out more about that man.' She decided to visit Viktor's **apartment** that Friday.

The **doorman** at the apartment building knew Vera. This wasn't her first visit, but she usually arrived together with Viktor and Angie.

'Hi, Jim,' she said. 'I have to take some designs from Viktor's apartment and he's away at the moment. Can you open the door for me, please? I have a key, but I left it at the office, I'm afraid.'

'Sure,' said the doorman. They took the **elevator** to Viktor's floor. Jim opened the door to Viktor's apartment with his key, and then went back downstairs in the elevator. 'What a piece of luck!' thought Vera.

fall autumn; the three months of the year before winter

apartment a number of rooms in a building where someone lives

doorman a man who looks after a building and watches the people who come in and out

elevator this takes people up and down to different floors in a building

closet a piece of furniture where you put things to wear

refrigerator a cold box for things to eat

She went inside and looked around. Viktor's apartment was cold and very tidy. The walls were white and all the things in the rooms were black or red or grey. Everything was in its place. In the living room, there were a lot of magazines. In Viktor's bedroom, the **closet** was full of modern and expensive black clothes. She went into the kitchen and opened the cupboards there. There was surprisingly little food. The **refrigerator** was nearly empty, too.

'That's strange,' said Vera. 'Doesn't this man eat?'

'Yes, I do. But I like different things from other people,' said a voice behind her. Vera turned round quickly.

Viktor was standing at the door, looking at her.

'Viktor! What are you doing here?' cried Vera.

'I live here, Vera,' he replied. 'Now, can I ask you the same question?'

Vera thought quickly.

'I needed a company magazine from last year,' she said. 'There weren't any of them at the office, and I know that you always keep some at your apartment. So I came to look for one here.'

Viktor laughed.

'Then why are you looking for it in the kitchen? It's OK. Don't lie. I know why you've come. You don't trust me, and you want to find out more about me.

Well, there's nothing here, so you can forget it. Do you know why I've come back a day early? I wanted to surprise Angie. I bought a ring for her in London. She's going to marry me, Vera. So you see, I've won and you've lost. Angie will never listen to you now because she's going to be my wife. She belongs to me.'

Vera gasped.

'You can't do this! You can't marry her! Soon after you came to Ballantine's, things began to happen – terrible things. Don died, then Sasha and Mylene. You're always there when there's an accident or a murder. Nobody can see it – only me! You don't love Angie, you're just using her.'

'You're wrong about that,' said Viktor coldly. 'I love Angie very much, and she loves me. We want to be together for the rest of our lives. Why can't you be happy for us? People ask too many questions. *You* ask too many questions. Be very careful and think before you speak, Vera. You can fight me – but you can never win against me!'

Viktor took off his dark glasses. He looked long and hard at Vera. His eyes were black and strangely empty of life. She suddenly felt very cold and afraid.

'Who *are* you, Viktor?' she asked, her voice shaking.

Viktor's face suddenly changed before her eyes, and he gave her his most charming smile.

'I'm the successful image consultant for Ballantine's, and soon I'll be the husband of Angie Ballantine, the beautiful face of our very successful company.'

Vera was **furious**. 'Yes – and you'll be very rich then, won't you, Viktor?' she said. 'Are you going to do something with that old family house in Bulgaria? It's falling down, isn't it? And your old housekeeper needs some help, too, doesn't she? Oh, yes – Angie's money will be very useful for all of that!'

Viktor looked back at her furiously for a minute, but then he smiled charmingly once more.

'Well, that's my business, isn't it? And if *you're* rich, Vera, it's because you're nothing but a thief! Please leave now before you say anything more. You can't stop me, Vera, because I know too much about you. The **wedding** is next week. Angie and I don't want to wait. She's happy and she needs me. So don't do anything to change that.'

Vera opened her mouth to speak, but she felt very afraid of Viktor now. She wanted to scream and shout, but she said nothing. There was something really **evil** about Viktor, but what was it? She still had no proof.

Silently, she turned round and walked out of the apartment. She could feel Viktor's cold eyes looking at the back of her neck while she was leaving.

Just when she reached the door, she felt a strong hand on her arm and she jumped.

'Don't forget what you came for, dear Vera,' said Viktor, and he gave her last year's company magazine.

When she was in the street again, she looked up at Viktor's window. She could see him standing there, watching her.

'This isn't the end of it,' Vera said to the dark figure. 'I'm not finished with you yet.'

Vera took her cell phone from her bag. 'Please tell me that it isn't true, Angie,' she said to herself. 'Please tell me that you're not going to marry Viktor.'

Angie answered the phone and said immediately, 'Oh good – it's you, Vera! I wanted to call you. I have some wonderful news. I'm going to marry Viktor! Please say that you're happy for me!'

So it was true. For a minute, Vera could not speak.

'Yes, I ... I know, Angie. I've just seen Viktor and he told me. It's wonderful news.'

'I'm so excited. I'm looking at wedding dresses now, but there are too many and I can't decide. I'm not even sure about the colour. What do you think – white, or grey, or maybe even red? Vera, you have to help me. I want to be beautiful on my wedding day. Can you come to the office? Maybe we can decide on my wedding dress together.'

'Yes,' answered Vera. 'Of course I'll help you, Angie. I'll be there in a few minutes.'

When she finished the call, Vera thought that she heard someone laughing evilly. The noise came from somewhere high above her.

READING CHECK

Are these sentences true or false? Tick the boxes.

		True	False
a	Vera looks at Viktor's computer to find out more about him.	☑	☐
b	Nobody on the Internet knows how old Viktor really is.	☐	☐
c	Vera opens Viktor's door with her key.	☐	☐
d	Vera has not been to Viktor's apartment before.	☐	☐
e	Viktor's apartment is very tidy.	☐	☐
f	There is very little food in Viktor's refrigerator.	☐	☐
g	Viktor comes back early from London.	☐	☐
h	Vera says that she is looking for some clothes.	☐	☐
i	Viktor has bought a dress for Angie.	☐	☐
j	Viktor tells Vera that he is going to marry Angie.	☐	☐
k	Angie is looking at wedding dresses.	☐	☐
l	Vera is really very happy for Angie.	☐	☐

WORD WORK

Use the words in the computer to complete Vera's diary on page 39.

apartment   closet   doorman

evil   ~~obsessed~~

elevator   screen

Internet   fall

furious   refrigerator

wedding

Thursday February 28th

I know that I'm becoming **a)** ...obsessed..., but I can't stop thinking about Viktor. He was away in London for the **b)** .... and winter fashion show so I stayed late at the office. I wanted to look at his computer to find out more about him. Of course, I didn't find anything because he's always very careful. After that, I used my computer to look on the **c)** .... A lot of news stories came up on the **d)** .... about Viktor and his time at Ballantine's. But nobody knows how old he really is – and that's very strange!

Then I hurried to Viktor's **e)** .... Jim, the **f)** ...., went up with me in the **g)** .... I lied about forgetting my key and Jim opened the door. I looked inside Viktor's **h)** ...., which was full of black clothes, and then I looked in the **i)** .... It was nearly empty. After that, everything went wrong. Viktor came back and told me that he's going to marry Angie. I was **j)** .... with him, but he just laughed. I called Angie and she says that it's true! She was looking at **k)** .... dresses and she wanted my help. I can't believe it! There's something very bad about Viktor. He's **l)** ...., but nobody believes me. What can I do?

GUESS WHAT

What do you think happens in the next chapter? Use the names of the people to complete the sentences.

Angie

Ed Valdemar

Viktor

Vera

a .... tells Vera about Don's letter.

b Viktor kisses .... on the neck.

c .... follows Vera to her apartment.

d Something terrible happens to ....

Chapter 7 – The wedding

guest a person that you invite to a wedding or a party

kiss to touch lovingly with your mouth

A week later, Angie married Viktor. She was very pale and beautiful in her long, white wedding dress. It was made by Ballantine's, of course. Ed Valdemar thought that Angie was too thin, but the other **guests** did not agree. Most of them worked for Ballantine's, and they thought that being very thin was really beautiful.

'Oh, she's so wonderful,' they all said. 'Like a world-famous model. Just right.'

After the wedding, there was a big party for all the guests in Angie's garden. At the party, Vera and Valdemar began talking.

'You're right, Ed. Of course she's too thin. I don't think that this wedding is good for her.'

'Hmmm, yes, maybe you're right. It's very soon after everything that's happened. But I think that it'll be the right thing for Angie in the end. Viktor loves her and he's very good for the company, too, you know.'

They looked across the garden at Viktor who had Angie in his arms. She was smiling, but her face was very tired, and there were dark circles under her eyes. Viktor, who was in his usual black clothes, was **kissing** her neck again and again hungrily.

'He's taking the life from her,' thought Vera. 'He's taking her blood, like a ... **vampire**. Yes, that was it – a vampire! But how can I think like this in the twenty-first **century**? I'm going crazy. Vampires belong to old stories about times long ago.'

'You're very quiet,' said Valdemar. 'Are you OK?'

'No, I'm not,' said Vera. 'I don't feel very well. I know that this wedding is a terrible mistake.'

Some of the other guests were listening to their conversation, and they turned and looked at Vera with shocked faces.

'She's jealous,' they said. 'She's jealous of Viktor's success, and she's angry because she isn't the most important person at Ballantine's now. That's why she's trying to **spoil** the wedding.'

Valdemar was angry with Vera, but he felt sorry for her, too.

'Look, Vera, you can't worry about this now. It's too late for that. Viktor did a **dumb** thing when he hit his head in the garage and said that it was you. But I think that he wanted Angie to feel sorry for him and to care for him. Sometimes we do dumb things when we're in love.'

vampire someone who died but comes back to life and who drinks the blood of living people to stay alive

century a hundred years

spoil to make something go wrong

dumb stupid, not thinking well

Vera looked at Valdemar. Her face was confused.

'What are you saying, Ed? How do you know that Viktor hit himself in the parking garage?'

'Don sent a letter to me before his accident. He saw Viktor hit himself on the CCTV camera recording, and he wanted to tell me about it. Don erased the recording because he was worried about Angie seeing it. He thought that maybe it wasn't so important, and I agreed. That's why I said nothing.'

Vera was furious. 'Not important? It's important to *me*! Viktor lied about that, and he lies about everything! He's evil! He's violent! I know that he killed Don! Maybe he killed Sasha and Mylene, too! Why didn't you tell me this before? What have you done, Ed? What's going to happen to Angie now?'

A lot of the guests standing around them were looking very uncomfortably at Vera now.

Valdemar took hold of Vera's arm with one big hand and he spoke to her quickly and quietly.

'Vera, please stop this crazy talk. It's Angie and Viktor's wedding day. I know that you're unhappy, but you mustn't do this. You're wrong about Viktor. He's good for Angie. Please don't spoil everything for them.'

'But you don't understand,' Vera said. 'Angie's in the most terrible danger.'

Vera pulled herself away from Valdemar and ran from the garden. Valdemar watched her go and shook his head sadly. 'Poor woman. She's been half crazy ever since George and Anne died so suddenly in that plane crash.'

Viktor looked up when Vera ran past him to the house. 'Excuse me,' he said to Angie and the guests who were near them. 'I must go into the house for a minute.'

He walked through the house to the front door, quickly opened it, and looked up the road. Yes! He could see Vera in the street. She was in a hurry, running to her apartment, which was not far from Angie's house.

Viktor followed Vera to her apartment building. She took the
elevator up to her floor – the 13th – and Viktor flew up the
stairs. His figure made a **shadow** on the wall like a huge bat.
Just after Vera opened the door to her apartment, Viktor came
up quickly behind her and pushed her inside.

Vera screamed and fell to the floor. Viktor put his hands round
her neck and looked hard into her face.

'You've gone too far this time,' he said coldly. 'You tried to spoil
Angie's wedding day!'

'You're crazy, Viktor,' screamed Vera. 'You're crazy and evil,
and you murdered Don – and poor Mylene and Sasha. I'm sure
of that now. Did you kill George and Anne, too? I need to know!'

'Yes, Vera, I did,' said Viktor. 'When I first read about Angie on
the Internet, I became obsessed with her. I knew that I wanted
her as my wife. I just needed to find a way to meet her. So I
decided to take a job at Ballantine's. George and Anne's deaths
were necessary for my plans to work. That's why I sent bats
into the engines of their plane and it crashed. The other deaths
just happened. They were people who began asking too many
questions and spoiling things. So they had to go.'

shadow a dark
shape that the
light makes behind
or under things

'But you're not just a murderer, are you?' gasped Vera while Viktor's hands closed around her neck. 'You're more than that. You're a vampire! And you're taking the life-blood from poor Angie's body! You're making her into a vampire, too!'

She put out her hand and pulled off Viktor's dark glasses. He smiled back at her, and Vera looked squarely into his face and saw the centuries of evil behind his cold, dead eyes.

She began to scream and scream. Viktor took her head in his strong hands and hit it violently against the floor time after time. He put his mouth to her neck and drank her blood thirstily.

At first, Vera fought back, her arms and legs moving wildly. Little by little, she began to move more weakly. Viktor hit her head one last time, and then he stood up and looked down at Vera's still body – now with no life in it at all.

He took her bag, opened it, and quickly threw all the things inside it onto the floor.

'You can't be too careful in New York, Vera,' he said. 'There are thieves and murderers everywhere.'

Then he put on his dark glasses and carefully washed Vera's dry blood from the corners of his mouth. After that, he opened the door and left the apartment. Minutes later, he was back once more in Angie's garden.

Angie was laughing with some of the guests. She saw Viktor and called out to him.

'Where have you been, **darling**? The party just isn't the same without you!'

Viktor came over and put his arm round his wife.

'I had to make a phone call about our **honeymoon**. I was asking for a special room in the hotel. I want only the best for my darling Mrs Sarav.'

The wedding guests smiled at Viktor. 'What a charming and caring man!' they thought. 'And he loves Angie so much! This is the wedding of the year. Ballantine's is a great success and we're all going to be rich!' One of the guests took his glass in his hand.

'To Viktor and Angie,' he said loudly, 'and to their wonderful future together.'

Everyone held up their glasses. 'To Viktor and Angie!' they all cried happily.

An hour later, Angie and Viktor got into their car to go to the airport. The guests went into the street to say goodbye to them. Angie smiled at all her friends.

'I haven't seen Vera for a while. I wanted to say goodbye to her. Do you know where she is, darling?' asked Angie.

'No. But don't worry about her. She's fine,' said Viktor. 'She told me today that she's very happy for us. We can put all our disagreements behind us now.'

'Oh, that's wonderful,' said Angie, touching his pale face with her fingers. 'I'm so lucky to have the two of you.'

darling something that you say to someone you love

honeymoon a vacation that two people take together just after they get married

READING CHECK

What do they say or think? Match the words with the people and the situations.

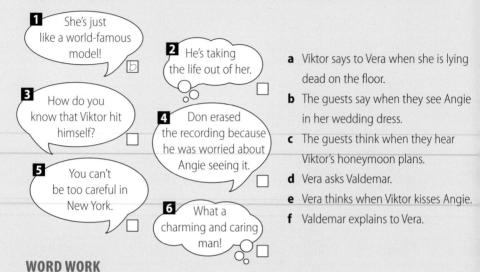

1 She's just like a world-famous model! b

2 He's taking the life out of her. ☐

3 How do you know that Viktor hit himself? ☐

4 Don erased the recording because he was worried about Angie seeing it. ☐

5 You can't be too careful in New York. ☐

6 What a charming and caring man! ☐

a Viktor says to Vera when she is lying dead on the floor.

b The guests say when they see Angie in her wedding dress.

c The guests think when they hear Viktor's honeymoon plans.

d Vera asks Valdemar.

e Vera thinks when Viktor kisses Angie.

f Valdemar explains to Vera.

WORD WORK

1 Find eight more words from Chapter 7 in the letter square.

K	I	S	S	G	H	I	Z	X	C	J
D	B	D	H	A	K	L	S	E	R	H
A	M	D	A	S	X	G	D	S	S	C
R	A	X	D	H	E	G	U	R	P	E
L	C	H	O	N	E	Y	M	O	O	N
I	B	V	W	K	F	D	B	Q	I	T
N	V	A	M	P	I	R	E	K	L	U
G	X	K	V	E	G	E	C	L	B	R
Z	N	G	U	E	S	T	Y	Q	U	Y

2 Complete the sentences with the correct form of the words in Activity 1 on page 46.

a After the wedding, John and Sandra went on their . . . . honeymoon . . to France.

b Dracula is a famous . . . .

c I'm sorry that I lied to you. Doing that was a really . . . . thing.

d There were over a hundred . . . . at the party.

e She was very loving to her husband and she always called him '. . . . . '.

f Maybe the bad weather will . . . . their wedding day.

g It's surprising that some people still believe in vampires in the twenty-first . . . .

h The sun is going down and the . . . . are becoming longer.

i I always . . . . my young children before they go to bed.

GUESS WHAT

What do you think happens to these three people in the next chapter?
Tick one box to finish each sentence.

a Angie . . .

    1 ☐ learns that Viktor is a vampire.

    2 ☐ goes to the Bahamas with Viktor.

    3 ☐ finds out that Vera is dead.

b Viktor . . .

    1 ☐ thinks about how he will make Angie into a vampire.

    2 ☐ goes swimming and does not come back.

    3 ☐ tells Angie that he does not love her.

c Vera . . .

    1 ☐ comes to the hotel to see Angie.

    2 ☐ calls Angie and tells her about Viktor.

    3 ☐ is on the TV news.

Chapter 8 – The honeymoon

vase you put flowers in this

balcony a place where you can sit or stand outside a building above the ground

ocean sea

juice water from fruit that you can drink

Angie and Viktor flew to the Bahamas for their honeymoon. Their hotel was a beautiful white building with a lot of tall, green trees all round it. Their rooms were very large, and they were full of **vases** of white and red flowers, which had a wonderful smell. Their **balcony** looked onto a beautiful white beach and the bright blue **ocean**.

'This is truly special, Viktor. Thank you so much,' said Angie, kissing her husband lovingly.

They took their clothes out of their suitcases and put them away in the closets. Then they changed out of their New York suits and put on summer clothes – all in Ballantine's colours of black, red, and grey.

Viktor looked in the refrigerator and took out two cold bottles of tomato **juice**. He made two long, red drinks, and brought them out onto the balcony. Angie was waiting for him there. They lay down side by side on long, white beach chairs, out of the sun. Both of them put on their dark glasses.

'Would you like to go swimming, my darling?' asked Viktor.

'Not today, thank you, darling. I need to rest after our journey here. Maybe tomorrow. Oh, why do I always feel so tired when I travel by plane? I mean, I'm just sitting in a plane seat for hours

– reading, eating, looking out of the window at the sky. What's so hard about that?'

'Are you *very* tired, my darling?' asked Viktor kindly.

'Yes, I am,' said Angie. 'But that's not surprising really. The wedding was so exciting. It *was* wonderful, wasn't it? Everyone was so kind. Of course, we'll need a bigger house for all the presents. But it all went so well, and I'm pleased about that.'

'Yes, my darling. You know, everyone at Ballantine's is very happy for both of us.'

'And I'm happy, too – but I can't stop thinking about Vera. Why hasn't she called me? Is she all right?'

'Don't worry about Vera, my darling. The days of my disagreements with her are finished now. Remember?'

'Yes, I remember. That's good.'

Just then, the news came on the large television in their hotel room. The sound was turned down, but from his beach chair, Viktor could see the television screen.

There were words travelling along the bottom of the screen, and he read them:

Famous fashion house partner dies fighting thief at home ...

'Yes,' Viktor thought, 'Vera died fighting all right!' She was a strong woman, and she did not go down quickly. Of course, as a vampire, he was stronger than her, but he really enjoyed killing Vera because she fought for her life. He really enjoyed drinking her blood, too. It was so exciting. She was a good rival!

Killing Don, and his mother and father – on the other hand – was boring. His bats did all the work for him then – flying into the engines of George's plane, hitting the windshield of Don's car. What was interesting about that?

Then there were Sasha and Mylene. Sasha once saw himself as a rival for Angie's love. What a poor, weak fool! Angie was far too good for him! And Mylene, as soon as she turned against Viktor, was so boring. He just had to kill them both to teach them a lesson.

Their deaths were very easy. He used his knife once for Sasha, and once for Mylene – and they fell to the ground without a sound. There was a lot of knife crime in the streets near that club. 'The police will be busy for a very long time trying to find Sasha and Mylene's murderer,' Viktor thought, and he laughed secretly inside himself.

He looked again at the TV screen. The words now on the screen were about Ballantine's:

*Fashion house **tragedy**. Sixth death* ...

'Ah well, no publicity is bad publicity!' thought Viktor. 'Of course, Vera's death is going to be hard on Angie. But with me at her side to help her, Angie's soon going to forget Vera Donato and feel happy again. I'll never tell her that Vera was a thief.

tragedy a very terrible thing that happens

50

My job now is to please Angie, and to help her
to stay happy – for centuries and centuries.'

He stood up and went into the room. He turned off
the television and took a white flower from one of the
vases. He walked back out onto the balcony and gave the
flower to his wife who smelled it, and put it in her hair.

They stood side by side together and looked out at the dark
blue ocean. The sky was beginning to go red and orange. The
shadows under the trees were darker and longer now.

'Ah,' he said. 'The sun's going down. This is my favourite time
of day. I'm a real "night bird", you know, Angie.'

'Me too,' said Angie. 'That's lucky, isn't it? I loved lying in the
sun when I was younger, but now I feel really uncomfortable

doing that. And of course, I need to be pale and interesting. A red nose just isn't right for a model in a fashion photo!'

She went back to sit on her beach chair, and Viktor went and sat down beside her.

'Angie, my darling, don't you understand? You're becoming a vampire. And vampires don't like bright sun,' he said silently to himself. Angie noticed the little smile at the corners of Viktor's thin mouth.

'Why are you smiling? What are you thinking about?' asked Angie.

'I'm thinking about our next vacation,' answered Viktor. 'Why don't we go to Bulgaria in the fall? You liked it there, and I haven't visited my house in Varna for a very long time. We can go after the next Paris fashion show.'

'What a good idea,' cried Angie. 'You know, I want to spend a lot of our money to make your old home beautiful again.'

'Me too,' said Viktor. 'And maybe this time you can meet some of my family in Varna.'

'Your family!' said Angie. 'But, Viktor, I didn't know that you had any of your family left there!'

'Oh, yes. I do,' replied Viktor. 'I come from an old Bulgarian family, you know – *very* old. The Saravs go back to the 16th century.'

'Then why didn't I meet any of them before?' Angie asked.

'You didn't meet them because I didn't think that it was a good idea – not before the wedding, you know,' explained Viktor. 'They're an *unusual* crowd, shall we say? But now you're my wife, and there's no turning back. I know that they'll be very pleased when they meet you in Varna! There's my sister, my three brothers, my mother and father, my grandmother on my mother's side of the family, my grandfather on my father's side, and *his* father, too. They'll be really happy when they learn that new American blood is coming into the Sarav family!'

The soft sound of the ocean under Viktor's voice was so restful, and Angie wasn't listening very carefully to her husband's words any more.

'Oh, good. That's nice,' she replied. 'Well, I really can't wait to meet all of them.'

She lay back on the beach chair and smiled happily. Viktor looked at her beautiful face, and the two small, red holes in her long, white neck. He suddenly felt thirsty for blood, but he decided to wait until later that evening to drink. He spoke silent words to Angie in his head.

'When you have your bath tonight, my darling, I'll go to you. I'll take all the blood from your body and I'll give you my vampire blood to drink. You won't die, my darling. You'll be born again before the morning as a full vampire, like me. And then – oh, then – we'll have all the time in the world to be together!'

READING CHECK

Correct the mistakes in the sentences.

a Viktor and Angie go to the ~~Maldives~~ *Bahamas* for their honeymoon.

b They drive there from New York.

c They change their names when they arrive at the hotel.

d Viktor makes two sandwiches for himself and Angie.

e Angie is worried because Ed hasn't called her.

f Viktor can see the radio from his beach chair.

g Viktor smiles because he didn't like killing Vera.

h Viktor used his dogs to kill Don and his parents.

i Viktor killed Sasha because he fell in love with Mylene.

j Viktor tells Angie that he has three sisters in Bulgaria.

k Angie agrees to go to Viktor's house to kill his family.

WORD WORK

Use words from Chapter 8 to correct the boxed words in these sentences.

a The Pacific is the biggest office ....ocean.... in the world.

b *Hamlet* is a famous travel .... by William Shakespeare.

c Can you put the flowers in that blue voice .... on the table?

d Drinking fruit jump .... is not as good for you as eating the fruit itself.

e Our hotel room has a big company .... looking out over the beach.

GUESS WHAT

What happens after the story ends? Choose from these ideas or add your own.

a ☐ Angie becomes a vampire and lives happily with Viktor in Bulgaria.

b ☐ Angie finds out about Vera's death and she kills Viktor angrily.

c ☐ Vera comes to life again as a vampire and she falls in love with Viktor.

d ☐ Angie does not become a vampire, but goes back to Ballantine's.

e ☐ ....

f ☐ ....

Project A *Famous vampire stories*

1 Read the text and write notes in the information table below. Use a dictionary to help you.

Carmilla is a novel by the Irish writer Sheridan Le Fanu. The book was first published in 1872. The story happens in Styria in Austria. It is about Laura, a young girl who lives in an old castle with her father. When she is six, Laura has a dream about a strange young woman who comes to her at night, and bites her, but she has no marks on her body the next day. Twelve years later, Carmilla, a mysterious young woman with dark hair, arrives at Laura's door after an accident on the road. The woman is just like the woman in Laura's dream. Laura does not know it, but Carmilla is a vampire. She is very beautiful, but she can change her human form and become a large, black cat. She has special vampire powers – for example, she can walk through walls. Like other vampires, she sleeps in a

Joseph Sheridan Le Fanu

coffin. While Carmilla is staying with her, Laura becomes ill and nearly dies. At the end of the story, Laura gets better after her father and his friends destroy Carmilla. Many movies about female vampires retell the Carmilla story.

Author of novel	
Name of vampire	
Name of novel	
Publication date	
Setting of story	
Vampire's victim(s)	
Description of vampire	
Animal form(s)	
Special powers	
Vampire habits	
End of story	

PROJECTS

Read the notes about another famous vampire story and complete the text below.

Author of novel	Bram Stoker
Name of vampire	Count Dracula
Name of novel	Dracula
Publication date	1897
Setting of story	Transylvania and England
Vampire's victim(s)	Lucy Westenra, Mina Harker
Description of vampire	tall, thin face, very pale, very strong
Animal form(s)	bat, wolf, large dog
Special powers	can see in the dark, can change the weather, and can run up walls
Vampire habits	sleeps in his coffin
End of story	Dracula returns to Transylvania, a group of Mina's friends go after him and destroy him

.... is a novel by the Irish writer .... The book was first published in .... In the book, the vampire .... travels from his home in .... across the sea by ship to .... There, he attacks .... and .... Stoker describes the count as a .... man with a .... face. He is very .... , but he is also very .... He can change from his human form into a .... , a .... , or a large .... He has special vampire powers too – for example, he can see well .... and he can change the .... round him. He can also .... walls like an insect. Like many vampires, he .... in his .... At the end of the story, ... returns to his castle in .... , but a group of .... friends follow him and .... him there. Many movies about vampires retell the .... story.

Do you know any other famous vampire stories in books or films? Research and write about one of them, using the texts in activities 1 and 2 to help you.

Project B   *A family crest*

1 Match the objects with the people from the story.

a — Viktor Sarav
b — Angie Ballantine
c — Vera Donato
d — Sasha Demidov
e — Ed Valdemar
f — Mylene Lavine

1 · 2 · 3 · 4 · 5 · 6

2 Read about Viktor's family crest and complete the table on page 59.

Viktor Sarav comes from an old Bulgarian family. The Saravs have a family crest. This is a picture that tells us about the history of a family.

Viktor's family crest has four symbols: a bat, a castle, a lion, and the moon. The bat means that the family are vampires. Viktor uses bats to kill George, Anne, and Don. The castle tells us that the family is rich and very old. The lion is a strong, confident animal, and the Saravs are strong, confident people. The moon tells us that the Saravs are people of the night. They are strongest at night when the moon is full.

Under the family crest, there is a motto. This is a short sentence which says something important about the family. Viktor's family motto is *Danger is Sweet*. What does this mean? We know that Viktor enjoys a fight. When his victims die easily, he is unhappy. So his family motto means that Viktor loves exciting things.

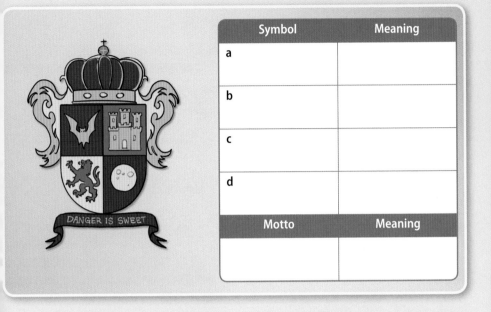

	Symbol	Meaning
a		
b		
c		
d		
	Motto	**Meaning**

3 Here is Mylene Lavine's family crest and notes about it. Read and complete the description of the crest on page 60.

	Symbol	Meaning
a	roll of cloth	colour and design
b	violin	love of music
c	sun	light
d	tree	enjoys life and the natural world
	Motto	**Meaning**
	Work Above All Things	You must work for the important things in life

59

Mylene Lavine comes from an old French Canadian .... Her family crest has four .... They are a .... of ...., a ...., the ...., and a .... The .... of .... stands for .... and .... Mylene works in fashion and these things are important to her. The .... means a .... of .... Many people in Mylene's family play musical instruments. The .... tells us that Mylene needs .... to live and work. And the .... means that Mylene enjoys .... and the ....

Mylene is a warm, friendly person. Her family .... is *Work Above All Things*. Mylene's family have always .... hard. She knows that she must work hard to get the .... things in life. But she enjoys her job and loves working at Ballantine's.

4 Match the mottoes with the people. Use a dictionary to help you.

a Ed Valdemar

b Vera Donato

c Angie Ballantine

d Sasha Demidov

1 *My face is my fortune*

2 *Protect the weak*

3 *Friends are forever*

4 *The law is above all things*

5 Choose a character from the story and invent a family crest for him or her. Follow these steps:

– Choose four symbols and explain their meaning.

– Choose a motto and explain its meaning.

– Draw the family crest.

GRAMMAR CHECK

Past Simple and Past Continuous

We use the Past Simple for finished past events. We use the Past Continuous for an activity that was in progress when events in the Past Simple happened. We use *was / were* + present participle to make the Past Continuous. We often use *when* to introduce the Past Simple verb and *while* to introduce the Past Continuous verb.

The Ballantines were flying over open country when their plane crashed.

The Ballantines' plane crashed while they were flying over open country.

With stative verbs – like feel, like, love, think, and want – we don't usually use the Past Continuous.

Angie ~~was having~~ a beautiful face. ✗   *Angie had a beautiful face.* ✔

1 Answer the questions about the beginning of the story. Use the words in brackets.

a What was Vera doing during the reading of the will? (look / a photograph of her friends)

.... She was looking at a photograph of her friends. ....

b What was Don doing? (hold / Angie's hand)

....

c How did Angie and Don feel? (feel / sad)

....

d What did Valdemar do while he was leaving? (think / plane accident)

....

e What were George and Anne doing in the photograph? (smile)

....

2 Put the verbs in brackets in the text into the Past Simple or the Past Continuous.

While Viktor **a)** .. was looking .. (look) on the Internet, he **b)** .... (see) a photo

of Angie. She **c)** .... (smile) beautifully at the camera. Viktor immediately

d) .... (fall) in love, and he **e)** .... (decide) that he wanted to marry her.

While he **f)** .... (work) for Ballantine's, Viktor quickly **g)** .... (become)

Vera's enemy. One day, he **h)** .... (come) into the office with a bandage

round his head. He **i)** .... (tell) Angie all about it when suddenly the phone

j) .... (ring). While Viktor **k)** .... (answer) the call, Don went to

look at the CCTV recording.

Direct speech and reported speech

In direct speech, we give the words that people say or think. In reported speech, we use a reporting verb (say, tell, ask, think, etc.) and we put the verb in direct speech one step back into the past. We also change the pronouns (I, you, etc.) and the possessive adjectives (my, our, etc.) We usually use that to introduce reported statements.

'I'm going to cry,' thought Angie.   *Angie thought that she was going to cry.*

'I can't tell anyone about Viktor!' said Vera.   *Vera said that she couldn't tell anyone about Viktor.*

When we report questions with the verb be, we change the order of the subject and verb. We use a question word – what, where, when – instead of that to introduce a reported information question.

'What are you doing, Vera?' asked Viktor. (= verb + subject)

Viktor asked Vera what she was doing. (= subject + verb)

3 Write these sentences as reported speech.

a 'Ballantine's is in your hands,' explained Valdemar.

<u>Valdemar explained that Ballantine's was in their hands.</u>

b 'Things don't change very much,' he said.

....

c 'We need to find some new people,' explained Vera.

....

....

d 'What are we going to do?' Angie asked Vera.

....

e 'I know important people, too,' said Don.

....

f 'Vera is a good worker,' thought Valdemar.

....

g 'Where are you going, Don?' asked Angie.

....

h 'I really want to help!' said Vera.

....

GRAMMAR

GRAMMAR CHECK

To + infinitive or –ing form of verb

After the verbs begin, enjoy, finish, go, go on, like, love, prefer, remember, and stop, we use verb + *–ing*.

Valdemar preferred living in New York to living in Stockholm.

After the verbs begin, decide, forget, learn, like, need, remember, try, want, and would like, we use *to* + infinitive.

Angie decided to work as a model.

With the verb remember, the meaning changes with *to* + infinitive or verb + *–ing*.

Don remembered to mail the letter.

(= the remembering is first and looks forward to the mailing)

Viktor remembered meeting Angie for the first time.

(= the remembering is second and looks back to the meeting)

With the verbs begin and like, the meaning does not change.

New people began to work / working at Ballantine's.

Sasha liked to design / designing women's clothes.

4 Complete these sentences about the story with the *to* + infinitive or verb + *–ing* form of the verb in brackets.

a A lot of people wanted ...to have... (have) a job at Ballantine's.

b Mylene liked .... (work) with Sasha.

c Viktor enjoyed .... (show) Angie's photo to the other workers.

d Everyone was excited when Viktor finished .... (speak).

e Angie couldn't stop .... (cry) after Don died.

f Vera needed .... (find out) more about Viktor.

g Vera was unhappy, but she went on .... (work) with Viktor.

h She began .... (look for) news about Viktor on his computer.

i She tried .... (find) something in Viktor's apartment.

j When she arrived at the door, she remembered .... (ask) Jim for the key.

k She remembered .... (steal) money from the company many years before.

l She forgot .... (take) one of the company magazines with her.

m Viktor learned .... (speak) English in Bulgaria.

63

GRAMMAR

GRAMMAR CHECK

Reflexive pronouns

We use reflexive pronouns (myself, yourself, himself, herself, itself, ourselves, yourselves, and themselves) when the subject and the object of a verb are the same.

He often asked himself about the accident.

Did the bat hurt itself on the windshield?

They told themselves that Angie was a wonderful model.

We can also use reflexive pronouns to emphasize who did something, or for things that a person does alone without anybody else.

Angie ate nothing herself.   *Viktor found the photo himself.*

5 Read Vera's diary. Complete the text with the words in the box.

herself	himself	himself	itself	~~myself~~
myself	ourselves	themselves	yourself	yourselves

Saturday October 20th

I often ask **a)** ....myself.... why George and Anne died in that plane crash. After all, George was flying the plane **b)** .... and it wasn't the first time. Valdemar and Don are asking **c)** .... the same question, I'm sure. Things aren't going well at Ballantine's. I don't trust Viktor. He came in yesterday with a bandage on his head saying, 'Someone hit me in the parking garage.' But I think that he maybe hurt **d)** .... He just wants Angie to feel sorry for him. Viktor isn't as important as he thinks. When he's away, we look after the business **e)** .... – and we do it well. We don't need him. Mylene and Sasha are very good workers. Of course, poor Angie spends all her time looking at **f)** .... in the mirror and asking, 'Can I really be a model?' She isn't confident at all. Dear Angie, please look after **g)** ....!

Tomorrow we're going to Milan so the New York office must look after **h)** .... for a while. I tell **i)** .... that everything will be all right, but I'm not sure. Mylene and Sasha, you must look after **j)** .... – and don't trust Viktor!

64

GRAMMAR

GRAMMAR CHECK

Modal auxiliary verbs: can, could, must, and have to

We use can (can't) / could (not) + infinitive without *to* to express ability, permission, or requests.

Vera couldn't run any faster. (= past ability) *He can speak Bulgarian.* (= general ability)

On Fridays, you can wear jeans at the office. (= permission)

Can / Could I ask you a question? (= request)

We use must (not) + infinitive without *to* for strong obligation or prohibition.

I must mail that letter. (= strong obligation) *You mustn't smoke here.* (= prohibition)

We use have to / don't have to + the infinitive when something is necessary / not necessary. *I have to leave.* *You don't have to answer me now.*

There is a big difference in meaning between don't have to and mustn't.

You don't have to do that. (= it's not necessary) *You mustn't do that.* (= it's not a good idea)

There is a small difference in meaning between have to and must.

I have to speak to him. (= obligation from outside the speaker)

I must speak to him. (= obligation from inside the speaker)

We use had to for inside and outside obligation in the past. *He had to leave.*

6 Choose the correct modal verb in these sentences.

a Vera wanted to tell everyone about Viktor, but she *couldn't* / *can't* .

b Viktor said, 'You *must* / *have* be very careful, Vera. I know too much about you.'

c 'I *have* / *can* to go back to New York,' said Viktor.

d 'We *don't have* / *mustn't* to visit Bulgaria,' said Vera to Angie. 'It's just one idea.'

e 'We *can't* / *haven't* visit Milan and not go shopping,' said Angie.

f '*Could* / *Have* I look at that magazine?' asked Angie.

7 Complete the text with suitable modal forms.

Don **a)** ..*couldn't*.. show Angie the CCTV camera recording because she wasn't very strong. But he **b)** .... look after her. 'I **c)** .... drive to her house,' he thought. 'We **d)** .... trust Viktor now. I **e)** .... believe that he hit his own head and said that it was Vera. Oh, why did our parents **f)** .... die in a crash? Before that, my poor sister **g)** .... laugh. Now, she is sad all the time. I **h)** .... forget to mail that letter to Valdemar. All of us **i)** .... be very careful in the future.

65

GRAMMAR

GRAMMAR CHECK

Tag endings with different tenses

We use question tags to check information, or to ask someone to agree with us. The tag contains a main verb or an auxiliary verb + a subject to match the sentence. When the sentence is affirmative, the question tag is negative. When the sentence is negative, the question tag is affirmative.

You can drive, can't you?   *You can't drive, can you?*

With most tenses, we repeat the main verb or auxiliary verb in the question tag.

He isn't a vampire, is he?   *She was afraid, wasn't she?*

Vera hasn't left, has she?   *We won't be late, will we?*

With affirmative Present Simple or Past Simple verbs, we use *do* or *did* in the question tag.

You like him, don't you?   *I left the computer on, didn't I?*

8 **What did Viktor say to Angie? Complete the questions with tag endings.**

  a You don't need to rest, ...*do you*....?

  b You'll be the face of Ballantine's, ...?

  c You aren't crying, ...?

  d We must go to Milan, ...?

  e We don't need to take Vera, ...?

  f You have everything, ...?

9 **What did Angie say to Viktor? Use the prompts to make sentences.**

  a you / love me

      ....*You love me, don't you*........?

  b we / not having / much luck

      ....?

  c Vera / be / good friend

      ....?

  d my shoes / not be / very nice

      ....?

  e you / have not talked / Valdemar recently

      ....?

  f you / be going / marry me

      ....?

66

GRAMMAR CHECK

Adjectives ending in –ing and –ed

We use adjectives ending in –*ing* to talk about things, events, and people that make us feel different things.

Viktor had a pleasing voice.

For Valdemar, the will was not so interesting.

We use adjectives ending in –*ed* to talk about how people feel.

Vera was interested in the will.

Everyone was pleased with Viktor's work.

10 Choose the correct words to complete the sentences.

a When Valdemar learned about his friends' plane crash, he was *surprised* / *surprising*.

b Vera thought that her job was very *interesting* / *interested*.

c Angie and Don felt *worried* / *worrying* about the future of Ballantine's.

d Viktor had some *exciting* / *excited* new ideas to help the company.

e After her brother's death, Angie felt *frightened* / *frightening* of the future.

f Maybe Don was *bored* / *boring* with his job at Ballantine's.

g For Angie, the idea of being a model was *frightened* / *frightening*.

h It was *surprised* / *surprising* that nobody knew how old Viktor really was.

i Angie was *interested* / *interesting* in going to Bulgaria.

j A long vacation in the same place can be *boring* / *bored*.

k Angie was *excited* / *exciting* because Viktor wanted to marry her.

l The terrible accidents were very *worried* / *worrying*.